50 American Soup Recipes for Home

By: Kelly Johnson

Table of Contents

- New England Clam Chowder
- Chicken Noodle Soup
- Tomato Soup
- Corn Chowder
- Broccoli Cheddar Soup
- Split Pea Soup
- Beef Stew
- Minestrone Soup
- French Onion Soup
- Potato Leek Soup
- Manhattan Clam Chowder
- Butternut Squash Soup
- Gumbo
- White Chicken Chili
- Lentil Soup
- Chicken Tortilla Soup
- Cream of Mushroom Soup
- Chili Con Carne
- Seafood Chowder
- Pumpkin Soup
- Vegetable Beef Soup
- Black Bean Soup
- Italian Wedding Soup
- Creamy Cauliflower Soup
- Beef and Barley Soup
- Chicken and Rice Soup
- Spinach and Artichoke Soup
- Broccoli Soup
- Creamy Tomato Basil Soup
- Sweet Potato Soup
- Chicken Pot Pie Soup
- Ham and Potato Soup
- Tortellini Soup
- Cabbage Soup
- Lemon Chicken Orzo Soup

- Wild Rice Soup
- Mushroom Bisque
- Taco Soup
- Zuppa Toscana
- Sausage and Lentil Soup
- Cuban Black Bean Soup
- Roasted Red Pepper Soup
- Carrot Ginger Soup
- Hungarian Mushroom Soup
- Egg Drop Soup
- Thai Coconut Soup
- Avgolemono Soup
- Navy Bean Soup
- Creamy Chicken and Mushroom Soup
- Hawaiian Beef Soup

New England Clam Chowder

Ingredients:

- 4 slices bacon, chopped
- 1 onion, finely chopped
- 2 celery stalks, finely chopped
- 3 tablespoons all-purpose flour
- 2 cups chicken broth or clam juice
- 2 cups milk
- 2 cups diced potatoes
- 2 cans (6.5 oz each) chopped clams, drained, juice reserved
- Salt and pepper to taste
- 1/2 teaspoon dried thyme
- 1 bay leaf
- 1 cup heavy cream
- Chopped fresh parsley (optional, for garnish)

Instructions:

1. In a large pot or Dutch oven, cook chopped bacon over medium heat until crispy. Remove bacon with a slotted spoon and set aside, leaving the bacon fat in the pot.
2. Add chopped onion and celery to the pot. Cook until softened, about 5-7 minutes.
3. Sprinkle flour over the vegetables and cook, stirring constantly, for 1-2 minutes to make a roux.
4. Gradually stir in chicken broth (or clam juice) and milk. Add diced potatoes, reserved clam juice, thyme, bay leaf, salt, and pepper. Bring to a boil, then reduce heat and simmer until potatoes are tender, about 10-15 minutes.
5. Stir in chopped clams and heavy cream. Simmer for an additional 5 minutes to heat through.
6. Taste and adjust seasoning if needed. Remove bay leaf before serving.
7. Ladle into bowls, garnish with crispy bacon and chopped parsley if desired, and serve hot.

Enjoy your New England Clam Chowder! It's perfect for a comforting meal, especially during colder months.

Chicken Noodle Soup

Ingredients:

- 1 tablespoon olive oil
- 1 onion, chopped
- 2 carrots, sliced
- 2 celery stalks, sliced
- 2 cloves garlic, minced
- 6 cups chicken broth
- 2 cups shredded cooked chicken
- 2 cups egg noodles
- 1 teaspoon dried thyme
- Salt and pepper to taste
- Chopped fresh parsley (optional, for garnish)

Instructions:

1. In a large pot or Dutch oven, heat olive oil over medium heat. Add chopped onion, sliced carrots, and sliced celery. Cook until vegetables are softened, about 5-7 minutes.
2. Add minced garlic and cook for another 1 minute until fragrant.
3. Pour in chicken broth and bring to a boil.
4. Stir in shredded cooked chicken, egg noodles, and dried thyme. Reduce heat to medium-low and simmer until noodles are tender, about 10-12 minutes.
5. Season with salt and pepper to taste.
6. Ladle into bowls, garnish with chopped parsley if desired, and serve hot.

This Chicken Noodle Soup is hearty, comforting, and perfect for any time of year. Enjoy!

Tomato Soup

Ingredients:

- 2 tablespoons butter
- 1 onion, chopped
- 2 cloves garlic, minced
- 2 tablespoons all-purpose flour
- 4 cups chicken or vegetable broth
- 2 cans (14.5 oz each) diced tomatoes
- 1 can (6 oz) tomato paste
- 1 teaspoon sugar
- 1/2 teaspoon dried basil
- 1/2 teaspoon dried oregano
- Salt and pepper to taste
- 1/2 cup heavy cream (optional, for a creamy version)
- Chopped fresh basil or parsley (optional, for garnish)

Instructions:

1. In a large pot or Dutch oven, melt butter over medium heat. Add chopped onion and cook until softened, about 5 minutes.
2. Add minced garlic and cook for another 1 minute until fragrant.
3. Sprinkle flour over the onions and garlic, stirring constantly, and cook for 1-2 minutes to make a roux.
4. Gradually whisk in chicken or vegetable broth, ensuring there are no lumps.
5. Stir in diced tomatoes (with their juices), tomato paste, sugar, dried basil, and dried oregano. Bring to a simmer.
6. Reduce heat to low and simmer uncovered for about 20-25 minutes, stirring occasionally, until flavors are blended and soup has slightly thickened.
7. If using, stir in heavy cream for a creamy tomato soup. Season with salt and pepper to taste.
8. Remove from heat and let cool slightly. If desired, use an immersion blender to puree the soup until smooth. Alternatively, blend in batches in a regular blender.
9. Ladle into bowls, garnish with chopped fresh basil or parsley if desired, and serve hot.

This Tomato Soup pairs wonderfully with grilled cheese sandwiches or a crusty bread for dipping. Enjoy!

Corn Chowder

Ingredients:

- 4 slices bacon, chopped
- 1 onion, chopped
- 2 celery stalks, chopped
- 2 carrots, chopped
- 2 cloves garlic, minced
- 4 cups chicken or vegetable broth
- 4 cups fresh or frozen corn kernels (about 6-8 ears of corn)
- 2 large potatoes, peeled and diced
- 1 teaspoon dried thyme
- 1/2 teaspoon smoked paprika (optional)
- Salt and pepper to taste
- 1 cup heavy cream
- Chopped fresh parsley or chives (optional, for garnish)

Instructions:

1. In a large pot or Dutch oven, cook chopped bacon over medium heat until crispy. Remove bacon with a slotted spoon and set aside, leaving the bacon fat in the pot.
2. Add chopped onion, celery, and carrots to the pot. Cook until vegetables are softened, about 5-7 minutes.
3. Add minced garlic and cook for another 1 minute until fragrant.
4. Pour in chicken or vegetable broth, scraping up any browned bits from the bottom of the pot.
5. Stir in corn kernels, diced potatoes, dried thyme, smoked paprika (if using), salt, and pepper. Bring to a boil, then reduce heat to medium-low and simmer uncovered until potatoes are tender, about 15-20 minutes.
6. Stir in heavy cream and simmer for an additional 5 minutes to heat through.
7. Taste and adjust seasoning if needed.
8. Ladle into bowls, garnish with crispy bacon and chopped fresh parsley or chives if desired, and serve hot.

This Corn Chowder is perfect for showcasing the flavors of summer corn and makes a satisfying meal on its own or paired with crusty bread. Enjoy!

Broccoli Cheddar Soup

Ingredients:

- 4 tablespoons butter
- 1 onion, chopped
- 2 cloves garlic, minced
- 1/4 cup all-purpose flour
- 4 cups chicken or vegetable broth
- 4 cups chopped fresh broccoli florets (about 2 medium heads)
- 2 cups shredded sharp cheddar cheese
- 1 cup heavy cream or half-and-half
- Salt and pepper to taste
- Pinch of nutmeg (optional)
- Chopped fresh chives or green onions (optional, for garnish)

Instructions:

1. In a large pot or Dutch oven, melt butter over medium heat. Add chopped onion and cook until softened, about 5 minutes.
2. Add minced garlic and cook for another 1 minute until fragrant.
3. Sprinkle flour over the onions and garlic, stirring constantly, and cook for 1-2 minutes to make a roux.
4. Gradually whisk in chicken or vegetable broth, ensuring there are no lumps.
5. Add chopped broccoli florets. Bring to a simmer and cook for about 10-15 minutes, until broccoli is tender.
6. Use an immersion blender to partially blend the soup to your desired consistency. Alternatively, transfer a portion of the soup to a blender and blend until smooth, then return to the pot.
7. Stir in shredded cheddar cheese until melted and smooth.
8. Stir in heavy cream or half-and-half. Season with salt, pepper, and a pinch of nutmeg if using.
9. Simmer for another 5 minutes to heat through and allow flavors to meld.
10. Ladle into bowls, garnish with chopped fresh chives or green onions if desired, and serve hot.

This Broccoli Cheddar Soup is rich, creamy, and packed with cheesy broccoli goodness. It pairs beautifully with crusty bread or a side salad. Enjoy!

Split Pea Soup

Ingredients:

- 1 tablespoon olive oil
- 1 onion, chopped
- 2 carrots, chopped
- 2 celery stalks, chopped
- 2 cloves garlic, minced
- 1 lb (about 2 cups) dried split peas, rinsed and drained
- 8 cups chicken or vegetable broth
- 1 bay leaf
- 1 teaspoon dried thyme
- Salt and pepper to taste
- 1 smoked ham hock or 1 cup diced ham (optional, for added flavor)
- Chopped fresh parsley (optional, for garnish)

Instructions:

1. In a large pot or Dutch oven, heat olive oil over medium heat. Add chopped onion, carrots, and celery. Cook until vegetables are softened, about 5-7 minutes.
2. Add minced garlic and cook for another 1 minute until fragrant.
3. Add dried split peas, chicken or vegetable broth, bay leaf, dried thyme, salt, and pepper. Stir to combine.
4. If using, add the smoked ham hock or diced ham to the pot for added flavor. Bring to a boil.
5. Reduce heat to low, cover, and simmer for about 1 to 1.5 hours, stirring occasionally, until split peas are tender and soup has thickened. If using a ham hock, remove it from the soup, shred the meat, and return it to the pot.
6. Taste and adjust seasoning with salt and pepper if needed.
7. Remove bay leaf before serving.
8. Ladle into bowls, garnish with chopped fresh parsley if desired, and serve hot.

This Split Pea Soup is delicious on its own or served with a slice of crusty bread. It's a comforting dish that's sure to warm you up. Enjoy!

Beef Stew

Ingredients:

- 2 lbs stew beef, cut into 1-inch cubes
- Salt and pepper to taste
- 1/4 cup all-purpose flour
- 2 tablespoons vegetable oil
- 1 onion, chopped
- 2 cloves garlic, minced
- 4 cups beef broth
- 1 cup red wine (optional)
- 2 bay leaves
- 1 teaspoon dried thyme
- 4 carrots, peeled and sliced
- 4 potatoes, peeled and diced
- 1 cup frozen peas (optional)
- Chopped fresh parsley (optional, for garnish)

Instructions:

1. Season stew beef cubes with salt and pepper. Dredge in all-purpose flour, shaking off excess.
2. In a large pot or Dutch oven, heat vegetable oil over medium-high heat. Add the beef cubes in batches and brown on all sides. Remove browned beef and set aside.
3. In the same pot, add chopped onion and cook until softened, about 5 minutes. Add minced garlic and cook for another 1 minute until fragrant.
4. Pour in beef broth and red wine (if using), scraping up any browned bits from the bottom of the pot.
5. Return browned beef cubes to the pot. Add bay leaves and dried thyme. Bring to a boil.
6. Reduce heat to low, cover, and simmer for about 1.5 to 2 hours, stirring occasionally, until beef is tender.
7. Add sliced carrots and diced potatoes. Cover and simmer for another 30-45 minutes, or until vegetables are tender and stew has thickened.
8. If using, add frozen peas in the last 5 minutes of cooking.
9. Taste and adjust seasoning with salt and pepper if needed. Remove bay leaves before serving.
10. Ladle into bowls, garnish with chopped fresh parsley if desired, and serve hot.

This Beef Stew is a complete meal in itself and is best enjoyed with crusty bread or over a bed of mashed potatoes. It's a comforting dish that's sure to satisfy. Enjoy!

Minestrone Soup

Ingredients:

- 2 tablespoons olive oil
- 1 onion, chopped
- 2 cloves garlic, minced
- 2 carrots, peeled and diced
- 2 celery stalks, diced
- 1 zucchini, diced
- 1 yellow squash, diced
- 1 cup green beans, trimmed and cut into 1-inch pieces
- 1 can (14 oz) diced tomatoes
- 6 cups vegetable or chicken broth
- 1 can (15 oz) cannellini beans, drained and rinsed
- 1 cup small pasta (such as ditalini or small shells)
- 1 teaspoon dried basil
- 1 teaspoon dried oregano
- Salt and pepper to taste
- Grated Parmesan cheese (optional, for serving)
- Chopped fresh basil or parsley (optional, for garnish)

Instructions:

1. In a large pot or Dutch oven, heat olive oil over medium heat. Add chopped onion and cook until softened, about 5 minutes.
2. Add minced garlic and cook for another 1 minute until fragrant.
3. Add diced carrots, celery, zucchini, yellow squash, and green beans. Cook for about 5 minutes, stirring occasionally, until vegetables begin to soften.
4. Stir in diced tomatoes (with their juices) and cook for another 2-3 minutes.
5. Pour in vegetable or chicken broth. Bring to a boil, then reduce heat to medium-low and simmer, uncovered, for about 15-20 minutes, or until vegetables are tender.
6. Add cannellini beans and small pasta. Cook for another 10 minutes, or until pasta is al dente.
7. Stir in dried basil, dried oregano, salt, and pepper. Taste and adjust seasoning if needed.
8. Ladle into bowls, garnish with grated Parmesan cheese and chopped fresh basil or parsley if desired, and serve hot.

Minestrone Soup is versatile and can be adjusted based on available vegetables and personal preferences. It's perfect for a comforting meal, especially with a side of crusty bread. Enjoy!

French Onion Soup

Ingredients:

- 4 tablespoons butter
- 4 large onions, thinly sliced
- 2 cloves garlic, minced
- 1 teaspoon sugar
- 1/2 cup dry white wine (optional)
- 6 cups beef broth
- 1 bay leaf
- 1 teaspoon dried thyme
- Salt and pepper to taste
- Baguette slices or crusty bread, toasted
- 2 cups shredded Gruyère cheese (or Swiss cheese)
- Chopped fresh parsley (optional, for garnish)

Instructions:

1. In a large pot or Dutch oven, melt butter over medium heat. Add thinly sliced onions and cook, stirring occasionally, until onions are caramelized and golden brown, about 30-40 minutes.
2. Stir in minced garlic and cook for another 1 minute until fragrant.
3. Sprinkle sugar over the onions and stir to combine. This helps in caramelizing the onions evenly.
4. If using, pour in dry white wine to deglaze the pot, scraping up any browned bits from the bottom.
5. Add beef broth, bay leaf, dried thyme, salt, and pepper. Bring to a simmer and cook uncovered for about 20-30 minutes to allow the flavors to meld.
6. Taste and adjust seasoning with salt and pepper if needed.
7. Preheat the oven broiler. Arrange oven-safe soup bowls or crocks on a baking sheet.
8. Ladle the hot soup into the bowls. Top each bowl with a few slices of toasted baguette or crusty bread.
9. Sprinkle shredded Gruyère cheese (or Swiss cheese) generously over the bread slices, covering the soup completely.
10. Place under the broiler for 2-3 minutes, or until the cheese is melted and bubbly and starts to brown slightly.
11. Carefully remove from the oven using oven mitts. Garnish with chopped fresh parsley if desired and serve hot.

French Onion Soup is best enjoyed immediately while the cheese is still gooey and the broth is piping hot. It's a comforting and flavorful soup that makes a perfect appetizer or light meal. Enjoy!

Potato Leek Soup

Ingredients:

- 4 tablespoons unsalted butter
- 4 leeks, white and light green parts only, thinly sliced
- 4 large potatoes, peeled and diced
- 4 cups chicken or vegetable broth
- 1 cup heavy cream
- Salt and pepper to taste
- Chopped chives or parsley (optional, for garnish)

Instructions:

1. In a large pot or Dutch oven, melt butter over medium heat. Add sliced leeks and cook, stirring occasionally, until softened, about 5-7 minutes.
2. Add diced potatoes to the pot and cook for another 5 minutes, stirring occasionally.
3. Pour in chicken or vegetable broth. Bring to a boil, then reduce heat to medium-low and simmer, uncovered, for about 20-25 minutes, or until potatoes are tender.
4. Remove pot from heat. Use an immersion blender to puree the soup until smooth. Alternatively, transfer soup in batches to a blender and blend until smooth, then return to the pot.
5. Stir in heavy cream. Season with salt and pepper to taste.
6. If the soup needs to be reheated, do so gently over low heat, stirring occasionally.
7. Ladle into bowls, garnish with chopped chives or parsley if desired, and serve hot.

Potato Leek Soup is wonderfully creamy and can be served as a starter or a light meal, especially when paired with crusty bread. It's a comforting dish that's perfect for any time of year. Enjoy!

Manhattan Clam Chowder

Ingredients:

- 4 slices bacon, chopped
- 1 onion, chopped
- 2 celery stalks, chopped
- 2 carrots, chopped
- 2 cloves garlic, minced
- 1 green bell pepper, chopped
- 1 can (28 oz) diced tomatoes
- 4 cups chicken or vegetable broth
- 2 cups diced potatoes
- 2 cans (6.5 oz each) chopped clams, drained, juice reserved
- 1 bay leaf
- 1 teaspoon dried thyme
- Salt and pepper to taste
- Chopped fresh parsley (optional, for garnish)

Instructions:

1. In a large pot or Dutch oven, cook chopped bacon over medium heat until crispy. Remove bacon with a slotted spoon and set aside, leaving the bacon fat in the pot.
2. Add chopped onion, celery, carrots, garlic, and green bell pepper to the pot. Cook until vegetables are softened, about 5-7 minutes.
3. Stir in diced tomatoes (with their juices) and cook for another 5 minutes.
4. Pour in chicken or vegetable broth, reserved clam juice, diced potatoes, bay leaf, dried thyme, salt, and pepper. Bring to a boil.
5. Reduce heat to medium-low and simmer, uncovered, for about 15-20 minutes, or until potatoes are tender.
6. Stir in chopped clams and simmer for another 5 minutes to heat through.
7. Taste and adjust seasoning with salt and pepper if needed.
8. Remove bay leaf before serving.
9. Ladle into bowls, garnish with crispy bacon and chopped fresh parsley if desired, and serve hot.

Manhattan Clam Chowder is lighter than its creamy counterpart but still hearty and full of flavor. It pairs well with crusty bread or oyster crackers. Enjoy this savory soup!

Butternut Squash Soup

Ingredients:

- 1 large butternut squash (about 3 lbs), peeled, seeded, and diced
- 2 tablespoons olive oil
- 1 onion, chopped
- 2 carrots, peeled and chopped
- 2 celery stalks, chopped
- 2 cloves garlic, minced
- 4 cups vegetable or chicken broth
- 1 teaspoon dried thyme
- 1/2 teaspoon ground cinnamon
- 1/4 teaspoon ground nutmeg
- Salt and pepper to taste
- 1/2 cup heavy cream (optional, for added creaminess)
- Toasted pumpkin seeds or croutons (optional, for garnish)

Instructions:

1. Preheat oven to 400°F (200°C). Place diced butternut squash on a baking sheet lined with parchment paper. Drizzle with olive oil and season with salt and pepper. Toss to coat evenly. Roast in the preheated oven for 30-35 minutes, or until squash is tender and lightly caramelized. Remove from oven and set aside.
2. In a large pot or Dutch oven, heat olive oil over medium heat. Add chopped onion, carrots, and celery. Cook until vegetables are softened, about 5-7 minutes.
3. Add minced garlic, dried thyme, ground cinnamon, and ground nutmeg. Cook for another 1 minute until fragrant.
4. Add roasted butternut squash to the pot. Pour in vegetable or chicken broth, ensuring it covers the vegetables. Bring to a boil, then reduce heat to medium-low and simmer, uncovered, for about 15-20 minutes, stirring occasionally.
5. Remove pot from heat. Use an immersion blender to puree the soup until smooth. Alternatively, transfer soup in batches to a blender and blend until smooth, then return to the pot.
6. Stir in heavy cream if using, and season with salt and pepper to taste. Heat gently over low heat if needed.
7. Ladle into bowls, garnish with toasted pumpkin seeds or croutons if desired, and serve hot.

This Butternut Squash Soup is velvety smooth with a hint of sweetness from the roasted squash and warmth from the spices. It's a comforting and nutritious soup that's sure to be a hit. Enjoy!

Gumbo

Ingredients:

For the Roux:

- 1/2 cup vegetable oil
- 1/2 cup all-purpose flour

For the Gumbo:

- 1 onion, chopped
- 1 green bell pepper, chopped
- 2 celery stalks, chopped
- 4 cloves garlic, minced
- 1 lb andouille sausage, sliced
- 1 lb chicken thighs, boneless and skinless, diced
- 6 cups chicken broth
- 1 can (14.5 oz) diced tomatoes
- 1 teaspoon dried thyme
- 1 teaspoon dried oregano
- 1 teaspoon paprika
- 1/2 teaspoon cayenne pepper (adjust to taste)
- Salt and pepper to taste
- 1 bay leaf
- 2 cups okra, sliced (fresh or frozen)
- Cooked white rice, for serving
- Chopped green onions, for garnish

Instructions:

1. **Make the Roux:**
   - In a large Dutch oven or heavy-bottomed pot, heat vegetable oil over medium heat. Gradually whisk in flour, stirring constantly to combine. Continue cooking and stirring the roux until it reaches a dark caramel color, similar to milk chocolate, about 30-40 minutes. Be careful not to burn it; adjust heat as needed.
2. **Prepare the Gumbo:**
   - Add chopped onion, green bell pepper, celery, and minced garlic to the roux. Cook, stirring frequently, for about 5-7 minutes until vegetables are softened.
   - Add sliced andouille sausage and diced chicken thighs to the pot. Cook, stirring occasionally, until chicken is no longer pink, about 5-7 minutes.
   - Stir in chicken broth, diced tomatoes (with their juices), dried thyme, dried oregano, paprika, cayenne pepper, salt, pepper, and bay leaf. Bring to a boil.
   - Reduce heat to low and simmer, uncovered, for about 1 hour, stirring occasionally, until flavors meld and chicken is tender.
   - Add sliced okra to the pot and simmer for another 15-20 minutes, or until okra is cooked through and gumbo thickens slightly. Adjust seasoning with salt, pepper, and cayenne pepper to taste.
   - Remove bay leaf before serving.

- Serve gumbo hot over cooked white rice. Garnish with chopped green onions.

Gumbo is a versatile dish that can include various meats, seafood, and vegetables. This recipe provides a rich and flavorful base, perfect for serving with rice to soak up all the delicious flavors. Enjoy your homemade gumbo!

White Chicken Chili

Ingredients:

- 1 tablespoon olive oil
- 1 onion, chopped
- 3 cloves garlic, minced
- 1 jalapeño pepper, seeded and finely chopped (optional, for heat)
- 1 teaspoon ground cumin
- 1/2 teaspoon dried oregano
- 1/2 teaspoon chili powder
- 1/4 teaspoon cayenne pepper (adjust to taste)
- Salt and pepper to taste
- 2 cups shredded cooked chicken (rotisserie chicken works well)
- 2 cans (15 oz each) white beans (such as cannellini or Great Northern), drained and rinsed
- 4 cups chicken broth
- 1 cup frozen corn kernels
- 1/2 cup heavy cream or sour cream
- Juice of 1 lime
- Chopped fresh cilantro (optional, for garnish)
- Sliced avocado (optional, for garnish)

Instructions:

1. In a large pot or Dutch oven, heat olive oil over medium heat. Add chopped onion and cook until softened, about 5 minutes.
2. Add minced garlic and chopped jalapeño (if using). Cook for another 1 minute until fragrant.
3. Stir in ground cumin, dried oregano, chili powder, cayenne pepper, salt, and pepper. Cook for 1-2 minutes to toast the spices.
4. Add shredded cooked chicken and white beans to the pot. Stir to combine.
5. Pour in chicken broth and bring to a boil. Reduce heat to medium-low and simmer, uncovered, for about 20-25 minutes, stirring occasionally.
6. Stir in frozen corn kernels and continue to simmer for another 5-10 minutes, until chili thickens slightly and corn is heated through.
7. Stir in heavy cream or sour cream and lime juice. Adjust seasoning with salt and pepper to taste.
8. Remove from heat and let chili sit for a few minutes to allow flavors to meld.
9. Ladle into bowls, garnish with chopped fresh cilantro and sliced avocado if desired, and serve hot.

White Chicken Chili is flavorful and creamy, with a hint of spice from the jalapeño and chili seasonings. It's perfect for cozy dinners and can be easily customized with your favorite toppings. Enjoy this comforting bowl of chili!

Lentil Soup

Ingredients:

- 1 tablespoon olive oil
- 1 onion, chopped
- 2 carrots, diced
- 2 celery stalks, diced
- 2 cloves garlic, minced
- 1 teaspoon ground cumin
- 1 teaspoon ground coriander
- 1/2 teaspoon smoked paprika
- 1 cup dried green or brown lentils, rinsed and picked over
- 4 cups vegetable or chicken broth
- 1 can (14.5 oz) diced tomatoes
- 2 bay leaves
- Salt and pepper to taste
- Fresh lemon juice (optional, for serving)
- Chopped fresh parsley or cilantro (optional, for garnish)

Instructions:

1. In a large pot or Dutch oven, heat olive oil over medium heat. Add chopped onion, diced carrots, and diced celery. Cook until vegetables are softened, about 5-7 minutes.
2. Add minced garlic, ground cumin, ground coriander, and smoked paprika. Cook for another 1-2 minutes until fragrant.
3. Stir in rinsed lentils, vegetable or chicken broth, diced tomatoes (with their juices), and bay leaves. Bring to a boil.
4. Reduce heat to medium-low and simmer, uncovered, for about 25-30 minutes, or until lentils are tender. Stir occasionally.
5. Season with salt and pepper to taste. If the soup is too thick, add more broth or water to reach your desired consistency.
6. Remove bay leaves before serving.
7. Optionally, squeeze fresh lemon juice into each bowl before serving for a bright citrus flavor.
8. Ladle into bowls, garnish with chopped fresh parsley or cilantro if desired, and serve hot.

Lentil Soup is nutritious, packed with protein and fiber from the lentils, and full of delicious flavors from the spices and vegetables. It's a comforting soup that pairs well with crusty bread or a side salad. Enjoy your homemade lentil soup!

Chicken Tortilla Soup

Ingredients:

- 1 tablespoon olive oil
- 1 onion, chopped
- 2 cloves garlic, minced
- 1 jalapeño pepper, seeded and finely chopped (optional, for heat)
- 1 red bell pepper, chopped
- 1 green bell pepper, chopped
- 1 teaspoon ground cumin
- 1 teaspoon chili powder
- 1/2 teaspoon paprika
- 1/4 teaspoon cayenne pepper (adjust to taste)
- Salt and pepper to taste
- 1 can (14.5 oz) diced tomatoes
- 6 cups chicken broth
- 1 lb boneless, skinless chicken breasts or thighs, cooked and shredded
- 1 can (15 oz) black beans, drained and rinsed
- 1 cup frozen corn kernels
- Juice of 1 lime
- Tortilla chips, crushed, for serving
- Shredded cheese, chopped fresh cilantro, sliced avocado, and sour cream, for garnish

Instructions:

1. In a large pot or Dutch oven, heat olive oil over medium heat. Add chopped onion and cook until softened, about 5 minutes.
2. Add minced garlic and chopped jalapeño (if using), red bell pepper, and green bell pepper. Cook for another 3-4 minutes until peppers are slightly softened.
3. Stir in ground cumin, chili powder, paprika, cayenne pepper, salt, and pepper. Cook for 1-2 minutes until fragrant.
4. Add diced tomatoes (with their juices) and chicken broth to the pot. Bring to a boil.
5. Reduce heat to medium-low and simmer, uncovered, for about 15-20 minutes, stirring occasionally.
6. Stir in shredded chicken, black beans, and frozen corn kernels. Simmer for another 10 minutes to heat through.
7. Stir in lime juice. Taste and adjust seasoning with salt, pepper, and additional lime juice if desired.
8. Ladle into bowls. Serve hot, garnished with crushed tortilla chips, shredded cheese, chopped fresh cilantro, sliced avocado, and a dollop of sour cream.

Chicken Tortilla Soup is a complete meal in itself, packed with protein, vegetables, and a delicious blend of spices. It's perfect for a cozy dinner or to warm up on a chilly day. Enjoy your homemade soup!

Cream of Mushroom Soup

Ingredients:

- 1/4 cup unsalted butter
- 1 onion, finely chopped
- 2 cloves garlic, minced
- 1 lb mushrooms (button or cremini), sliced
- 1/4 cup all-purpose flour
- 4 cups chicken or vegetable broth
- 1 cup heavy cream
- Salt and pepper to taste
- Fresh thyme leaves (optional, for garnish)
- Sliced mushrooms, sautéed until golden (optional, for garnish)

Instructions:

1. In a large pot or Dutch oven, melt butter over medium heat. Add finely chopped onion and cook until softened, about 5 minutes.
2. Add minced garlic and sliced mushrooms to the pot. Cook, stirring occasionally, until mushrooms are tender and golden brown, about 8-10 minutes.
3. Sprinkle flour over the mushrooms and stir to coat evenly. Cook for 1-2 minutes, stirring constantly.
4. Gradually pour in chicken or vegetable broth, stirring constantly to prevent lumps from forming.
5. Bring the mixture to a simmer, then reduce heat to low. Let it simmer for about 15-20 minutes, stirring occasionally, until the soup thickens slightly.
6. Stir in heavy cream and continue to simmer for another 5 minutes, or until heated through.
7. Season with salt and pepper to taste.
8. Remove from heat. If desired, use an immersion blender to blend some of the soup for a creamier texture, leaving some mushroom pieces intact.
9. Ladle into bowls, garnish with fresh thyme leaves and sautéed sliced mushrooms if desired, and serve hot.

Cream of Mushroom Soup is perfect on its own or as a starter for a meal. It pairs wonderfully with crusty bread or a side salad. Enjoy your homemade soup!

Chili Con Carne

Ingredients:

- 2 tablespoons olive oil
- 1 onion, chopped
- 3 cloves garlic, minced
- 1 jalapeño pepper, seeded and finely chopped (optional, for heat)
- 1 lb ground beef (preferably lean)
- 1 can (14.5 oz) diced tomatoes
- 2 tablespoons tomato paste
- 2 cups beef broth
- 1 can (15 oz) kidney beans, drained and rinsed
- 1 can (15 oz) black beans, drained and rinsed
- 2 teaspoons ground cumin
- 2 teaspoons chili powder
- 1 teaspoon paprika
- 1/2 teaspoon dried oregano
- 1/4 teaspoon cayenne pepper (adjust to taste)
- Salt and pepper to taste
- Chopped fresh cilantro, for garnish
- Shredded cheese, sour cream, diced avocado, and sliced jalapeños, for serving (optional)

Instructions:

1. In a large pot or Dutch oven, heat olive oil over medium heat. Add chopped onion and cook until softened, about 5 minutes.
2. Add minced garlic and chopped jalapeño (if using). Cook for another 1-2 minutes until fragrant.
3. Add ground beef to the pot. Cook, breaking up the meat with a spoon, until browned and cooked through, about 5-7 minutes.
4. Stir in diced tomatoes (with their juices) and tomato paste. Cook for 2-3 minutes, stirring occasionally.
5. Pour in beef broth, kidney beans, black beans, ground cumin, chili powder, paprika, dried oregano, cayenne pepper, salt, and pepper. Stir to combine.
6. Bring the mixture to a boil, then reduce heat to medium-low. Simmer, uncovered, for about 30-40 minutes, stirring occasionally, until chili has thickened and flavors have melded.
7. Taste and adjust seasoning with salt, pepper, and additional chili powder or cayenne pepper if desired.
8. Remove from heat. Serve hot, garnished with chopped fresh cilantro. Optionally, serve with shredded cheese, sour cream, diced avocado, and sliced jalapeños on the side.

Chili Con Carne is delicious on its own or served over rice. It's a comforting and satisfying dish, perfect for gatherings or cozy meals at home. Enjoy your homemade chili!

Seafood Chowder

Ingredients:

- 4 slices bacon, chopped
- 1 onion, chopped
- 2 celery stalks, chopped
- 2 carrots, diced
- 2 cloves garlic, minced
- 1/4 cup unsalted butter
- 1/4 cup all-purpose flour
- 4 cups seafood or fish broth
- 2 cups milk (whole milk or half-and-half)
- 2 cups diced potatoes
- 1 bay leaf
- 1/2 teaspoon dried thyme
- Salt and pepper to taste
- 1 lb mixed seafood (such as shrimp, scallops, and/or firm white fish), peeled, deveined, and cut into bite-sized pieces
- 1 cup frozen corn kernels
- 1/2 cup heavy cream
- Chopped fresh parsley, for garnish
- Oyster crackers or crusty bread, for serving

Instructions:

1. In a large pot or Dutch oven, cook chopped bacon over medium heat until crispy. Remove bacon with a slotted spoon and set aside, leaving the bacon fat in the pot.
2. Add chopped onion, celery, carrots, and minced garlic to the pot. Cook until vegetables are softened, about 5-7 minutes.
3. Add unsalted butter to the pot and let it melt. Sprinkle all-purpose flour over the vegetables and stir to combine, cooking for 1-2 minutes to make a roux.
4. Gradually pour in seafood or fish broth and milk, stirring constantly to prevent lumps. Add diced potatoes, bay leaf, dried thyme, salt, and pepper.
5. Bring the mixture to a simmer and cook uncovered for about 15-20 minutes, or until potatoes are tender and the soup has thickened slightly.
6. Stir in mixed seafood (shrimp, scallops, and/or fish) and frozen corn kernels. Simmer for another 5-7 minutes, or until seafood is cooked through.
7. Stir in heavy cream and adjust seasoning with salt and pepper to taste.
8. Remove bay leaf before serving.
9. Ladle into bowls, garnish with chopped fresh parsley and crispy bacon pieces. Serve hot with oyster crackers or crusty bread.

Seafood Chowder is a comforting and hearty soup that's perfect for a cozy dinner or a special occasion. It's creamy, flavorful, and packed with delicious seafood flavors. Enjoy your homemade seafood chowder!

Pumpkin Soup

Ingredients:

- 2 tablespoons unsalted butter
- 1 onion, chopped
- 2 cloves garlic, minced
- 1 teaspoon ground cumin
- 1/2 teaspoon ground coriander
- 1/4 teaspoon ground cinnamon
- 1/8 teaspoon ground nutmeg
- 1/8 teaspoon cayenne pepper (optional, for a hint of heat)
- 4 cups pumpkin puree (canned or homemade)
- 4 cups vegetable or chicken broth
- 1 cup coconut milk (full-fat, for creaminess)
- Salt and pepper to taste
- 1 tablespoon maple syrup or honey (optional, for sweetness)
- Toasted pumpkin seeds, for garnish
- Fresh cilantro or parsley, chopped, for garnish

Instructions:

1. In a large pot or Dutch oven, melt butter over medium heat. Add chopped onion and cook until softened, about 5 minutes.
2. Add minced garlic, ground cumin, ground coriander, ground cinnamon, ground nutmeg, and cayenne pepper (if using). Cook for another 1-2 minutes until fragrant.
3. Add pumpkin puree and vegetable or chicken broth to the pot. Stir to combine.
4. Bring the mixture to a boil, then reduce heat to medium-low and simmer, uncovered, for about 15-20 minutes, stirring occasionally.
5. Stir in coconut milk and season with salt and pepper to taste. If you prefer a sweeter soup, stir in maple syrup or honey at this point.
6. Using an immersion blender, blend the soup until smooth. Alternatively, carefully transfer the soup in batches to a blender and blend until smooth, then return to the pot.
7. Taste and adjust seasoning if needed.
8. Serve hot, garnished with toasted pumpkin seeds and chopped fresh cilantro or parsley.

Pumpkin Soup is creamy, velvety, and packed with warm spices that complement the natural sweetness of the pumpkin. It's perfect for a cozy autumn or winter evening. Enjoy your homemade pumpkin soup!

Vegetable Beef Soup

Ingredients:

- 1 tablespoon olive oil
- 1 lb beef stew meat, cut into bite-sized pieces
- Salt and pepper to taste
- 1 onion, chopped
- 2 cloves garlic, minced
- 2 carrots, peeled and diced
- 2 celery stalks, diced
- 1 bell pepper (any color), chopped
- 1 can (14.5 oz) diced tomatoes
- 6 cups beef broth
- 2 cups diced potatoes
- 1 cup frozen corn kernels
- 1 cup frozen peas
- 1 teaspoon dried thyme
- 1 teaspoon dried oregano
- 1 bay leaf
- Salt and pepper to taste
- Chopped fresh parsley or cilantro, for garnish

Instructions:

1. In a large pot or Dutch oven, heat olive oil over medium-high heat. Season beef stew meat with salt and pepper. Add meat to the pot and cook until browned on all sides, about 5-7 minutes. Remove meat from pot and set aside.
2. In the same pot, add chopped onion, minced garlic, diced carrots, diced celery, and chopped bell pepper. Cook, stirring occasionally, until vegetables are softened, about 5 minutes.
3. Add diced tomatoes (with their juices) and beef broth to the pot. Stir to combine.
4. Return browned beef stew meat to the pot. Add diced potatoes, frozen corn kernels, frozen peas, dried thyme, dried oregano, and bay leaf. Stir well.
5. Bring the mixture to a boil, then reduce heat to medium-low and simmer, uncovered, for about 30-40 minutes, or until beef is tender and vegetables are cooked through. Stir occasionally.
6. Season with salt and pepper to taste.
7. Remove bay leaf before serving.
8. Ladle into bowls, garnish with chopped fresh parsley or cilantro, and serve hot.

Vegetable Beef Soup is a comforting and nutritious meal that's packed with tender beef, hearty vegetables, and flavorful broth. It's perfect for a satisfying lunch or dinner. Enjoy your homemade vegetable beef soup!

Black Bean Soup

Ingredients:

- 2 tablespoons olive oil
- 1 onion, chopped
- 2 cloves garlic, minced
- 1 jalapeño pepper, seeded and finely chopped (optional, for heat)
- 2 teaspoons ground cumin
- 1 teaspoon chili powder
- 1/2 teaspoon smoked paprika
- 1/4 teaspoon cayenne pepper (adjust to taste)
- Salt and pepper to taste
- 3 cans (15 oz each) black beans, drained and rinsed
- 4 cups vegetable or chicken broth
- 1 can (14.5 oz) diced tomatoes
- Juice of 1 lime
- 1/2 cup fresh cilantro, chopped (plus extra for garnish)
- Sour cream or Greek yogurt, for garnish
- Sliced green onions, for garnish
- Tortilla chips or strips, for serving

Instructions:

1. In a large pot or Dutch oven, heat olive oil over medium heat. Add chopped onion and cook until softened, about 5 minutes.
2. Add minced garlic and chopped jalapeño (if using). Cook for another 1-2 minutes until fragrant.
3. Stir in ground cumin, chili powder, smoked paprika, cayenne pepper, salt, and pepper. Cook for 1-2 minutes until spices are fragrant.
4. Add 2 cans of drained and rinsed black beans to the pot, along with vegetable or chicken broth and diced tomatoes (with their juices). Stir to combine.
5. Bring the mixture to a boil, then reduce heat to medium-low and simmer, uncovered, for about 15-20 minutes, stirring occasionally.
6. Using an immersion blender, blend the soup until smooth. Alternatively, transfer a portion of the soup to a blender and blend until smooth, then return to the pot.
7. Stir in the remaining can of black beans (drained and rinsed), lime juice, and chopped cilantro. Simmer for another 5 minutes to heat through.
8. Taste and adjust seasoning with salt, pepper, and additional lime juice if desired.
9. Serve hot, garnished with a dollop of sour cream or Greek yogurt, sliced green onions, chopped fresh cilantro, and tortilla chips or strips on the side.

Black Bean Soup is delicious on its own or served with toppings for added texture and flavor. It's a comforting and nutritious dish that's perfect for any time of the year. Enjoy your homemade black bean soup!

Italian Wedding Soup

Ingredients:

For the Meatballs:

- 1/2 lb ground pork
- 1/2 lb ground beef
- 1/2 cup breadcrumbs
- 1/4 cup grated Parmesan cheese
- 1 egg
- 2 cloves garlic, minced
- 1 tablespoon fresh parsley, chopped
- Salt and pepper to taste

For the Soup:

- 1 tablespoon olive oil
- 1 onion, finely chopped
- 2 carrots, diced
- 2 celery stalks, diced
- 2 cloves garlic, minced
- 8 cups chicken broth
- 1 bay leaf
- 1 teaspoon dried oregano
- 1 teaspoon dried thyme
- Salt and pepper to taste
- 2 cups small pasta (such as ditalini or orzo)
- 4 cups fresh spinach or kale, chopped
- Grated Parmesan cheese, for serving

Instructions:

1. **Prepare the Meatballs:**
   - In a bowl, combine ground pork, ground beef, breadcrumbs, grated Parmesan cheese, egg, minced garlic, chopped parsley, salt, and pepper.
   - Mix until well combined, then shape into small meatballs, about 1 inch in diameter.
2. **Cook the Meatballs:**
   - Heat olive oil in a large pot over medium heat. Add meatballs and cook until browned on all sides, about 5-7 minutes. Remove meatballs from the pot and set aside.
3. **Prepare the Soup:**
   - In the same pot, add chopped onion, diced carrots, and diced celery. Cook until vegetables are softened, about 5 minutes.
   - Add minced garlic and cook for another 1-2 minutes until fragrant.
4. **Simmer the Soup:**
   - Pour in chicken broth and add bay leaf, dried oregano, dried thyme, salt, and pepper. Bring to a boil.
   - Add small pasta to the pot and cook according to package instructions until al dente.
5. **Finish the Soup:**

        - Stir in chopped spinach or kale and cooked meatballs. Simmer for another 5-7 minutes until greens are wilted and meatballs are heated through.
6. **Serve:**
        - Remove bay leaf before serving. Taste and adjust seasoning if needed.
        - Ladle soup into bowls and sprinkle with grated Parmesan cheese.

Italian Wedding Soup is hearty, comforting, and perfect for a satisfying meal. Enjoy this delicious soup with its tender meatballs, flavorful broth, and nutritious greens!

Creamy Cauliflower Soup

Ingredients:

- 1 large head of cauliflower, chopped into florets
- 2 tablespoons olive oil
- 1 onion, chopped
- 2 cloves garlic, minced
- 4 cups vegetable or chicken broth
- 1 cup milk (whole milk or half-and-half)
- Salt and pepper to taste
- Pinch of nutmeg (optional, for extra flavor)
- Chopped fresh chives or parsley, for garnish
- Grated Parmesan cheese, for garnish (optional)

Instructions:

1. In a large pot or Dutch oven, heat olive oil over medium heat. Add chopped onion and cook until softened, about 5 minutes.
2. Add minced garlic and cook for another 1-2 minutes until fragrant.
3. Add cauliflower florets to the pot and sauté for 5 minutes, stirring occasionally.
4. Pour in vegetable or chicken broth, enough to cover the cauliflower. Bring to a boil, then reduce heat to medium-low and simmer, covered, for about 15-20 minutes or until cauliflower is tender.
5. Using an immersion blender, blend the soup until smooth and creamy. Alternatively, carefully transfer the soup in batches to a blender and blend until smooth, then return to the pot.
6. Stir in milk (whole milk or half-and-half) and season with salt, pepper, and a pinch of nutmeg if using. Stir well to combine and heat through.
7. Taste and adjust seasoning if needed.
8. Serve hot, garnished with chopped fresh chives or parsley and grated Parmesan cheese if desired.

Creamy Cauliflower Soup is rich, velvety, and packed with flavor. It's a comforting soup that pairs well with crusty bread or a simple salad. Enjoy your homemade creamy cauliflower soup!

Beef and Barley Soup

Ingredients:

- 1 tablespoon olive oil
- 1 lb stew beef, cut into bite-sized pieces
- Salt and pepper to taste
- 1 onion, chopped
- 2 carrots, diced
- 2 celery stalks, diced
- 2 cloves garlic, minced
- 8 cups beef broth
- 1 cup pearl barley, rinsed
- 1 can (14.5 oz) diced tomatoes
- 1 bay leaf
- 1 teaspoon dried thyme
- 1 teaspoon dried rosemary
- Salt and pepper to taste
- Chopped fresh parsley, for garnish

Instructions:

1. In a large pot or Dutch oven, heat olive oil over medium-high heat. Season stew beef with salt and pepper. Add beef to the pot and cook until browned on all sides, about 5-7 minutes. Remove beef from pot and set aside.
2. In the same pot, add chopped onion, diced carrots, and diced celery. Cook until vegetables are softened, about 5 minutes.
3. Add minced garlic and cook for another 1-2 minutes until fragrant.
4. Pour in beef broth and scrape up any browned bits from the bottom of the pot. Add pearl barley, diced tomatoes (with their juices), bay leaf, dried thyme, dried rosemary, salt, and pepper. Stir well to combine.
5. Return browned beef to the pot. Bring the mixture to a boil, then reduce heat to medium-low and simmer, uncovered, for about 1 hour or until beef is tender and barley is cooked through, stirring occasionally.
6. Taste and adjust seasoning with salt and pepper if needed.
7. Remove bay leaf before serving.
8. Ladle into bowls, garnish with chopped fresh parsley, and serve hot.

Beef and Barley Soup is a comforting and nutritious meal that's perfect for a hearty lunch or dinner. Enjoy the rich flavors of tender beef, hearty barley, and aromatic herbs in this homemade soup!

Chicken and Rice Soup

Ingredients:

- 1 tablespoon olive oil
- 1 lb boneless, skinless chicken breasts or thighs, cut into bite-sized pieces
- Salt and pepper to taste
- 1 onion, chopped
- 2 carrots, diced
- 2 celery stalks, diced
- 2 cloves garlic, minced
- 8 cups chicken broth
- 1 cup white rice (long-grain or basmati)
- 1 bay leaf
- 1 teaspoon dried thyme
- 1/2 teaspoon dried rosemary
- 1/2 teaspoon dried oregano
- Salt and pepper to taste
- Chopped fresh parsley, for garnish
- Lemon wedges, for serving (optional)

Instructions:

1. In a large pot or Dutch oven, heat olive oil over medium-high heat. Season chicken pieces with salt and pepper. Add chicken to the pot and cook until browned on all sides, about 5-7 minutes. Remove chicken from pot and set aside.
2. In the same pot, add chopped onion, diced carrots, and diced celery. Cook until vegetables are softened, about 5 minutes.
3. Add minced garlic and cook for another 1-2 minutes until fragrant.
4. Pour in chicken broth and scrape up any browned bits from the bottom of the pot. Add white rice, bay leaf, dried thyme, dried rosemary, dried oregano, salt, and pepper. Stir well to combine.
5. Return browned chicken to the pot. Bring the mixture to a boil, then reduce heat to medium-low and simmer, covered, for about 15-20 minutes or until rice is cooked and chicken is tender, stirring occasionally.
6. Taste and adjust seasoning with salt and pepper if needed.
7. Remove bay leaf before serving.
8. Ladle into bowls, garnish with chopped fresh parsley, and serve hot with lemon wedges on the side for squeezing over the soup, if desired.

Chicken and Rice Soup is a comforting and nourishing meal that's easy to make and full of flavor. Enjoy the warmth and heartiness of this homemade soup!

Spinach and Artichoke Soup

Ingredients:

- 2 tablespoons unsalted butter
- 1 onion, chopped
- 2 cloves garlic, minced
- 1 can (14 oz) artichoke hearts, drained and chopped
- 4 cups vegetable or chicken broth
- 1 cup heavy cream
- 1 cup milk (whole milk or half-and-half)
- 4 cups fresh spinach leaves, chopped
- 1 cup grated Parmesan cheese
- Salt and pepper to taste
- Pinch of nutmeg (optional, for extra flavor)
- Red pepper flakes, for garnish (optional)
- Crusty bread or breadsticks, for serving

Instructions:

1. In a large pot or Dutch oven, melt butter over medium heat. Add chopped onion and cook until softened, about 5 minutes.
2. Add minced garlic and cook for another 1-2 minutes until fragrant.
3. Stir in chopped artichoke hearts and cook for 2-3 minutes.
4. Pour in vegetable or chicken broth, heavy cream, and milk. Stir to combine.
5. Bring the mixture to a simmer, then reduce heat to medium-low.
6. Add chopped spinach leaves to the pot and simmer for 5-7 minutes, until spinach is wilted and tender.
7. Stir in grated Parmesan cheese and season with salt, pepper, and a pinch of nutmeg if using. Stir well to combine and heat through.
8. Taste and adjust seasoning if needed.
9. Serve hot, garnished with a sprinkle of red pepper flakes if desired. Serve with crusty bread or breadsticks on the side.

Spinach and Artichoke Soup is creamy, rich, and packed with delicious flavors. It's a perfect soup for a cozy meal at home. Enjoy your homemade spinach and artichoke soup!

Broccoli Soup

Ingredients:

- 2 tablespoons unsalted butter
- 1 onion, chopped
- 2 cloves garlic, minced
- 1 potato, peeled and diced
- 4 cups broccoli florets (about 2 small heads of broccoli)
- 4 cups vegetable or chicken broth
- 1 cup milk (whole milk or half-and-half)
- Salt and pepper to taste
- Pinch of nutmeg (optional, for extra flavor)
- Grated cheddar cheese, for garnish (optional)
- Croutons or crusty bread, for serving

Instructions:

1. In a large pot or Dutch oven, melt butter over medium heat. Add chopped onion and cook until softened, about 5 minutes.
2. Add minced garlic and cook for another 1-2 minutes until fragrant.
3. Add diced potato and broccoli florets to the pot. Stir to combine.
4. Pour in vegetable or chicken broth. Bring to a boil, then reduce heat to medium-low and simmer, covered, for about 15-20 minutes, or until vegetables are tender.
5. Using an immersion blender, blend the soup until smooth and creamy. Alternatively, carefully transfer the soup in batches to a blender and blend until smooth, then return to the pot.
6. Stir in milk (whole milk or half-and-half) and season with salt, pepper, and a pinch of nutmeg if using. Stir well to combine and heat through.
7. Taste and adjust seasoning if needed.
8. Serve hot, garnished with grated cheddar cheese if desired, and accompanied by croutons or crusty bread.

Broccoli Soup is hearty, creamy, and full of flavor. It's a comforting soup that's perfect for a satisfying meal. Enjoy your homemade broccoli soup!

Creamy Tomato Basil Soup

Ingredients:

- 2 tablespoons olive oil
- 1 onion, chopped
- 2 cloves garlic, minced
- 1 can (28 oz) crushed tomatoes
- 2 cups vegetable or chicken broth
- 1/2 cup heavy cream
- 1/4 cup chopped fresh basil leaves
- 1 teaspoon dried oregano
- 1/2 teaspoon dried thyme
- Salt and pepper to taste
- Grated Parmesan cheese, for garnish (optional)
- Croutons or crusty bread, for serving

Instructions:

1. In a large pot or Dutch oven, heat olive oil over medium heat. Add chopped onion and cook until softened, about 5 minutes.
2. Add minced garlic and cook for another 1-2 minutes until fragrant.
3. Stir in crushed tomatoes, vegetable or chicken broth, dried oregano, and dried thyme. Bring to a simmer.
4. Reduce heat to medium-low and simmer, uncovered, for about 15-20 minutes, stirring occasionally.
5. Using an immersion blender, blend the soup until smooth. Alternatively, carefully transfer the soup in batches to a blender and blend until smooth, then return to the pot.
6. Stir in heavy cream and chopped fresh basil. Season with salt and pepper to taste.
7. Simmer for another 5 minutes to heat through and allow flavors to blend.
8. Taste and adjust seasoning if needed.
9. Serve hot, garnished with grated Parmesan cheese if desired, and accompanied by croutons or crusty bread.

Creamy Tomato Basil Soup is velvety, comforting, and perfect for dipping with crusty bread or enjoying on its own. It's a delightful soup that's sure to warm you up. Enjoy your homemade creamy tomato basil soup!

Sweet Potato Soup

Ingredients:

- 2 tablespoons olive oil
- 1 onion, chopped
- 2 cloves garlic, minced
- 2 large sweet potatoes, peeled and diced
- 1 carrot, peeled and diced
- 4 cups vegetable or chicken broth
- 1 can (14 oz) coconut milk (full-fat for creaminess)
- 1 teaspoon ground cumin
- 1/2 teaspoon ground cinnamon
- 1/4 teaspoon ground nutmeg
- Salt and pepper to taste
- Fresh cilantro or parsley, chopped, for garnish

Instructions:

1. In a large pot or Dutch oven, heat olive oil over medium heat. Add chopped onion and cook until softened, about 5 minutes.
2. Add minced garlic and cook for another 1-2 minutes until fragrant.
3. Add diced sweet potatoes and carrot to the pot. Cook for 5 minutes, stirring occasionally.
4. Pour in vegetable or chicken broth and coconut milk. Stir to combine.
5. Add ground cumin, ground cinnamon, and ground nutmeg. Stir well to incorporate.
6. Bring the mixture to a boil, then reduce heat to medium-low and simmer, covered, for about 20-25 minutes or until sweet potatoes and carrots are tender.
7. Using an immersion blender, blend the soup until smooth. Alternatively, carefully transfer the soup in batches to a blender and blend until smooth, then return to the pot.
8. Season with salt and pepper to taste.
9. Serve hot, garnished with chopped fresh cilantro or parsley.

Sweet Potato Soup is creamy, flavorful, and packed with warm spices that complement the natural sweetness of the sweet potatoes. It's a comforting soup that's perfect for a satisfying meal. Enjoy your homemade sweet potato soup!

Chicken Pot Pie Soup

Ingredients:

- 2 tablespoons unsalted butter
- 1 onion, chopped
- 2 cloves garlic, minced
- 2 carrots, diced
- 2 celery stalks, diced
- 1 lb boneless, skinless chicken breasts or thighs, diced
- 1/3 cup all-purpose flour
- 4 cups chicken broth
- 1 cup milk (whole milk or half-and-half)
- 1 cup frozen peas
- 1 cup frozen corn kernels
- 1 teaspoon dried thyme
- 1/2 teaspoon dried sage
- Salt and pepper to taste
- 1 sheet of puff pastry, thawed if frozen
- Chopped fresh parsley, for garnish

Instructions:

1. In a large pot or Dutch oven, melt butter over medium heat. Add chopped onion and cook until softened, about 5 minutes.
2. Add minced garlic, diced carrots, and diced celery. Cook for another 5 minutes, stirring occasionally.
3. Add diced chicken to the pot and cook until chicken is no longer pink, about 5-7 minutes.
4. Sprinkle flour over the chicken and vegetables. Stir well to coat everything evenly and cook for 1-2 minutes, stirring constantly.
5. Gradually pour in chicken broth and milk, stirring constantly to prevent lumps from forming.
6. Add frozen peas, frozen corn kernels, dried thyme, dried sage, salt, and pepper. Stir well to combine.
7. Bring the mixture to a boil, then reduce heat to medium-low and simmer, uncovered, for about 15-20 minutes or until soup has thickened and vegetables are tender.
8. While the soup is simmering, preheat your oven according to the puff pastry package instructions.
9. Cut the puff pastry sheet into squares or rounds, depending on your preference. Place them on a baking sheet lined with parchment paper.
10. Bake the puff pastry according to package instructions until golden brown and puffed.
11. Ladle the hot soup into bowls. Top each bowl with a piece of puff pastry.
12. Garnish with chopped fresh parsley and serve hot.

Chicken Pot Pie Soup is creamy, hearty, and filled with comforting flavors. Enjoy the combination of tender chicken, vegetables, and flaky puff pastry in this delicious soup!

Ham and Potato Soup

Ingredients:

- 2 tablespoons unsalted butter
- 1 onion, chopped
- 2 cloves garlic, minced
- 2 carrots, diced
- 2 celery stalks, diced
- 3 cups potatoes, peeled and diced
- 2 cups cooked ham, diced
- 4 cups chicken broth
- 1 cup milk (whole milk or half-and-half)
- 1 bay leaf
- 1 teaspoon dried thyme
- Salt and pepper to taste
- Chopped fresh parsley, for garnish

Instructions:

1. In a large pot or Dutch oven, melt butter over medium heat. Add chopped onion and cook until softened, about 5 minutes.
2. Add minced garlic, diced carrots, and diced celery. Cook for another 5 minutes, stirring occasionally.
3. Add diced potatoes and diced ham to the pot. Stir to combine.
4. Pour in chicken broth and add bay leaf and dried thyme. Stir well.
5. Bring the mixture to a boil, then reduce heat to medium-low and simmer, uncovered, for about 15-20 minutes or until potatoes are tender.
6. Stir in milk (whole milk or half-and-half). Season with salt and pepper to taste.
7. Simmer for another 5 minutes to heat through and allow flavors to blend.
8. Taste and adjust seasoning if needed.
9. Remove bay leaf before serving.
10. Ladle into bowls, garnish with chopped fresh parsley, and serve hot.

Ham and Potato Soup is a comforting and filling meal that's perfect for chilly days. Enjoy the hearty combination of tender potatoes, savory ham, and flavorful broth in this homemade soup!

Tortellini Soup

Ingredients:

- 1 tablespoon olive oil
- 1 onion, chopped
- 2 cloves garlic, minced
- 2 carrots, diced
- 2 celery stalks, diced
- 6 cups chicken or vegetable broth
- 1 can (14 oz) diced tomatoes
- 1 teaspoon dried basil
- 1 teaspoon dried oregano
- 1/2 teaspoon dried thyme
- Salt and pepper to taste
- 9 oz package of refrigerated or frozen cheese tortellini
- 4 cups fresh spinach leaves
- Grated Parmesan cheese, for garnish (optional)
- Chopped fresh basil or parsley, for garnish (optional)

Instructions:

1. In a large pot or Dutch oven, heat olive oil over medium heat. Add chopped onion and cook until softened, about 5 minutes.
2. Add minced garlic, diced carrots, and diced celery. Cook for another 5 minutes, stirring occasionally.
3. Pour in chicken or vegetable broth and diced tomatoes (with their juices). Add dried basil, dried oregano, dried thyme, salt, and pepper. Stir well to combine.
4. Bring the mixture to a boil, then reduce heat to medium-low and simmer, uncovered, for about 10 minutes to allow flavors to meld.
5. Add cheese tortellini to the pot and cook according to package instructions (usually about 7-9 minutes for refrigerated tortellini, or as directed for frozen tortellini), until tortellini are tender.
6. Stir in fresh spinach leaves and cook for another 1-2 minutes until spinach is wilted.
7. Taste and adjust seasoning with salt and pepper if needed.
8. Remove from heat.
9. Serve hot, garnished with grated Parmesan cheese and chopped fresh basil or parsley if desired.

Tortellini Soup is a delicious and comforting meal that's quick to prepare and full of flavor. Enjoy the combination of cheesy tortellini, hearty vegetables, and aromatic herbs in this homemade soup!

Cabbage Soup

Ingredients:

- 2 tablespoons olive oil
- 1 onion, chopped
- 2 cloves garlic, minced
- 4 cups cabbage, thinly sliced
- 2 carrots, diced
- 2 celery stalks, diced
- 1 potato, peeled and diced
- 6 cups vegetable or chicken broth
- 1 can (14 oz) diced tomatoes
- 1 teaspoon dried thyme
- 1 bay leaf
- Salt and pepper to taste
- Fresh parsley, chopped, for garnish

Instructions:

1. In a large pot or Dutch oven, heat olive oil over medium heat. Add chopped onion and cook until softened, about 5 minutes.
2. Add minced garlic and cook for another 1-2 minutes until fragrant.
3. Stir in thinly sliced cabbage, diced carrots, diced celery, and diced potato. Cook for about 5 minutes, stirring occasionally.
4. Pour in vegetable or chicken broth and add diced tomatoes (with their juices). Stir well to combine.
5. Add dried thyme, bay leaf, salt, and pepper. Stir again.
6. Bring the mixture to a boil, then reduce heat to medium-low and simmer, uncovered, for about 20-25 minutes or until vegetables are tender.
7. Taste and adjust seasoning with salt and pepper if needed.
8. Remove bay leaf before serving.
9. Ladle into bowls, garnish with chopped fresh parsley, and serve hot.

Cabbage Soup is a comforting and satisfying meal that's perfect for a chilly day. Enjoy the hearty combination of cabbage, vegetables, and savory broth in this homemade soup!

Lemon Chicken Orzo Soup

Ingredients:

- 1 tablespoon olive oil
- 1 onion, chopped
- 2 carrots, diced
- 2 celery stalks, diced
- 2 cloves garlic, minced
- 6 cups chicken broth
- 1 lb boneless, skinless chicken breasts or thighs, cut into bite-sized pieces
- 1/2 cup orzo pasta
- Zest and juice of 1-2 lemons (depending on taste)
- 1 teaspoon dried thyme
- Salt and pepper to taste
- Fresh parsley, chopped, for garnish

Instructions:

1. In a large pot or Dutch oven, heat olive oil over medium heat. Add chopped onion, diced carrots, and diced celery. Cook until vegetables are softened, about 5-7 minutes.
2. Add minced garlic and cook for another 1-2 minutes until fragrant.
3. Pour in chicken broth and bring to a boil.
4. Add chicken pieces and orzo pasta to the pot. Reduce heat to medium-low and simmer, uncovered, for about 10-15 minutes or until chicken is cooked through and orzo is tender.
5. Stir in lemon zest, lemon juice, dried thyme, salt, and pepper. Taste and adjust seasoning if needed.
6. Remove from heat.
7. Serve hot, garnished with chopped fresh parsley.

Lemon Chicken Orzo Soup is light, tangy, and full of comforting flavors. Enjoy the combination of tender chicken, hearty orzo pasta, and refreshing lemon in this homemade soup!

Wild Rice Soup

Ingredients:

- 1 tablespoon olive oil
- 1 onion, chopped
- 2 carrots, diced
- 2 celery stalks, diced
- 8 oz mushrooms, sliced
- 1 cup wild rice, rinsed
- 6 cups vegetable or chicken broth
- 1 lb boneless, skinless chicken breasts or thighs, diced (optional)
- 1 teaspoon dried thyme
- 1 bay leaf
- Salt and pepper to taste
- 1 cup heavy cream (optional, for a creamy soup)
- Fresh parsley, chopped, for garnish

Instructions:

1. In a large pot or Dutch oven, heat olive oil over medium heat. Add chopped onion, diced carrots, and diced celery. Cook until vegetables are softened, about 5-7 minutes.
2. Add sliced mushrooms to the pot and cook for another 5 minutes, stirring occasionally.
3. Stir in wild rice and cook for 1-2 minutes, stirring frequently.
4. Pour in vegetable or chicken broth. Add diced chicken (if using), dried thyme, bay leaf, salt, and pepper. Stir well to combine.
5. Bring the mixture to a boil, then reduce heat to medium-low and simmer, covered, for about 45-50 minutes or until wild rice is tender and cooked through.
6. If using heavy cream, stir it in during the last 10 minutes of cooking.
7. Taste and adjust seasoning with salt and pepper if needed.
8. Remove bay leaf before serving.
9. Serve hot, garnished with chopped fresh parsley.

Wild Rice Soup is rich, hearty, and full of delicious flavors. Enjoy the comforting combination of wild rice, vegetables, and optional chicken in this homemade soup!

Mushroom Bisque

Ingredients:

- 2 tablespoons unsalted butter
- 1 onion, chopped
- 2 cloves garlic, minced
- 1 lb mushrooms (such as cremini or button), sliced
- 1/4 cup all-purpose flour
- 4 cups vegetable or chicken broth
- 1 cup heavy cream
- 1/4 teaspoon dried thyme
- Salt and pepper to taste
- Fresh parsley, chopped, for garnish

Instructions:

1. In a large pot or Dutch oven, melt butter over medium heat. Add chopped onion and cook until softened, about 5 minutes.
2. Add minced garlic and sliced mushrooms to the pot. Cook for about 8-10 minutes, stirring occasionally, until mushrooms are softened and browned.
3. Sprinkle flour over the mushrooms and stir well to coat.
4. Gradually pour in vegetable or chicken broth, stirring constantly to prevent lumps from forming.
5. Bring the mixture to a boil, then reduce heat to medium-low and simmer, uncovered, for about 15-20 minutes, stirring occasionally, until soup has thickened slightly.
6. Stir in heavy cream and dried thyme. Season with salt and pepper to taste.
7. Simmer for another 5 minutes to heat through and allow flavors to blend.
8. Taste and adjust seasoning if needed.
9. Remove from heat.
10. Using an immersion blender, blend the soup until smooth and creamy. Alternatively, carefully transfer the soup in batches to a blender and blend until smooth, then return to the pot.
11. Serve hot, garnished with chopped fresh parsley.

Mushroom Bisque is creamy, velvety, and full of robust mushroom flavor. Enjoy the luxurious taste and texture of this homemade soup!

Taco Soup

Ingredients:

- 1 lb ground beef or turkey
- 1 onion, chopped
- 2 cloves garlic, minced
- 1 can (15 oz) black beans, drained and rinsed
- 1 can (15 oz) kidney beans, drained and rinsed
- 1 can (15 oz) corn kernels, drained
- 1 can (14.5 oz) diced tomatoes
- 1 can (10 oz) diced tomatoes with green chilies (like Rotel)
- 1 packet (1 oz) taco seasoning mix
- 4 cups beef or chicken broth
- Salt and pepper to taste
- Optional toppings: shredded cheese, sour cream, chopped cilantro, sliced jalapeños, tortilla chips

Instructions:

1. In a large pot or Dutch oven, cook ground beef or turkey over medium-high heat until browned and cooked through, breaking it up with a spoon as it cooks.
2. Add chopped onion and minced garlic to the pot. Cook for another 3-5 minutes until onion is softened and translucent.
3. Stir in black beans, kidney beans, corn kernels, diced tomatoes, diced tomatoes with green chilies, and taco seasoning mix. Mix well to combine.
4. Pour in beef or chicken broth. Stir to combine all ingredients.
5. Bring the mixture to a boil, then reduce heat to medium-low and simmer, uncovered, for about 20-25 minutes, stirring occasionally.
6. Taste and season with salt and pepper as needed.
7. Serve hot, garnished with your favorite toppings such as shredded cheese, sour cream, chopped cilantro, sliced jalapeños, and tortilla chips.

Taco Soup is flavorful, hearty, and packed with Tex-Mex-inspired goodness. Enjoy the robust flavors of tacos in this comforting and easy-to-make soup!

Zuppa Toscana

Ingredients:

- 1 lb Italian sausage (spicy or mild), casings removed
- 1 onion, chopped
- 3 cloves garlic, minced
- 4 cups chicken broth
- 3 cups water
- 3-4 medium potatoes, peeled and diced
- 1 bunch kale, stems removed and leaves chopped
- 1 cup heavy cream
- Salt and pepper to taste
- Red pepper flakes (optional, for added heat)
- Grated Parmesan cheese, for serving

Instructions:

1. In a large pot or Dutch oven, cook the Italian sausage over medium-high heat, breaking it up into smaller pieces with a spoon as it cooks. Cook until browned and cooked through, then remove from the pot and set aside.
2. In the same pot, add chopped onion and cook for 5 minutes, until softened. Add minced garlic and cook for another minute until fragrant.
3. Pour in chicken broth and water. Add diced potatoes to the pot. Bring to a boil, then reduce heat to medium-low and simmer, uncovered, for about 10-15 minutes, or until potatoes are tender.
4. Stir in cooked sausage and chopped kale. Simmer for another 5 minutes, until kale is wilted and tender.
5. Stir in heavy cream and season with salt, pepper, and red pepper flakes (if using) to taste.
6. Simmer for another 5 minutes to heat through and allow flavors to blend.
7. Taste and adjust seasoning if needed.
8. Serve hot, garnished with grated Parmesan cheese.

Zuppa Toscana is a hearty and comforting soup that's perfect for a cozy meal. Enjoy the rich flavors of Italian sausage, potatoes, and kale in this delicious homemade soup!

Sausage and Lentil Soup

Ingredients:

- 1 tablespoon olive oil
- 1 lb Italian sausage (spicy or mild), casings removed
- 1 onion, chopped
- 2 carrots, diced
- 2 celery stalks, diced
- 3 cloves garlic, minced
- 1 cup brown or green lentils, rinsed
- 6 cups chicken or vegetable broth
- 1 can (14.5 oz) diced tomatoes
- 1 teaspoon dried thyme
- 1 bay leaf
- Salt and pepper to taste
- Fresh parsley, chopped, for garnish

Instructions:

1. In a large pot or Dutch oven, heat olive oil over medium heat. Add Italian sausage and cook, breaking it up into smaller pieces with a spoon, until browned and cooked through. Remove sausage from the pot and set aside.
2. In the same pot, add chopped onion, diced carrots, and diced celery. Cook for about 5 minutes, until vegetables are softened.
3. Add minced garlic and cook for another minute until fragrant.
4. Stir in rinsed lentils, chicken or vegetable broth, diced tomatoes (with their juices), dried thyme, and bay leaf. Bring to a boil.
5. Reduce heat to medium-low and simmer, uncovered, for about 25-30 minutes, or until lentils are tender.
6. Stir in cooked sausage and simmer for another 5 minutes to heat through.
7. Season with salt and pepper to taste.
8. Remove bay leaf before serving.
9. Ladle into bowls, garnish with chopped fresh parsley, and serve hot.

Sausage and Lentil Soup is hearty, comforting, and packed with protein and fiber. Enjoy the robust flavors of sausage and lentils in this homemade soup!

Cuban Black Bean Soup

Ingredients:

- 2 tablespoons olive oil
- 1 onion, chopped
- 1 green bell pepper, chopped
- 1 red bell pepper, chopped
- 3 cloves garlic, minced
- 2 teaspoons ground cumin
- 1 teaspoon dried oregano
- 1/2 teaspoon ground coriander
- 1/4 teaspoon cayenne pepper (optional, for heat)
- 4 cups cooked black beans (about 3 cans, drained and rinsed)
- 4 cups vegetable or chicken broth
- 1 can (14.5 oz) diced tomatoes
- Juice of 1 lime
- Salt and pepper to taste
- Fresh cilantro, chopped, for garnish
- Sour cream or Greek yogurt, for serving (optional)

Instructions:

1. In a large pot or Dutch oven, heat olive oil over medium heat. Add chopped onion, green bell pepper, and red bell pepper. Cook for about 5-7 minutes, until vegetables are softened.
2. Add minced garlic, ground cumin, dried oregano, ground coriander, and cayenne pepper (if using). Cook for another 1-2 minutes, until fragrant.
3. Stir in cooked black beans, vegetable or chicken broth, and diced tomatoes (with their juices). Bring to a boil.
4. Reduce heat to medium-low and simmer, uncovered, for about 20-25 minutes, stirring occasionally.
5. Using an immersion blender, blend part of the soup until smooth to thicken, leaving some beans and vegetables whole for texture. Alternatively, transfer a portion of the soup to a blender and blend until smooth, then return to the pot.
6. Stir in lime juice. Season with salt and pepper to taste.
7. Simmer for another 5 minutes to allow flavors to blend.
8. Taste and adjust seasoning if needed.
9. Serve hot, garnished with chopped fresh cilantro and a dollop of sour cream or Greek yogurt if desired.

Cuban Black Bean Soup is savory, spicy (if you opt for cayenne), and filled with wholesome ingredients. Enjoy the vibrant flavors of this comforting soup!

Roasted Red Pepper Soup

Ingredients:

- 4 large red bell peppers
- 2 tablespoons olive oil
- 1 onion, chopped
- 2 cloves garlic, minced
- 4 cups vegetable or chicken broth
- 1 can (14.5 oz) diced tomatoes
- 1 teaspoon smoked paprika
- 1/2 teaspoon dried thyme
- Salt and pepper to taste
- 1/2 cup heavy cream (optional, for a creamy soup)
- Fresh basil or parsley, chopped, for garnish

Instructions:

1. Preheat the oven to 400°F (200°C). Place red bell peppers on a baking sheet and roast them in the oven for 30-35 minutes, turning occasionally, until the skins are charred and blistered. Remove from the oven and place in a bowl. Cover the bowl with plastic wrap or a damp towel and let the peppers steam for 10 minutes. This will make it easier to peel the skins off.
2. Once cooled, peel off the charred skins from the peppers, remove the seeds and stems, and roughly chop the flesh.
3. In a large pot or Dutch oven, heat olive oil over medium heat. Add chopped onion and cook until softened, about 5 minutes.
4. Add minced garlic and cook for another minute until fragrant.
5. Stir in roasted red peppers, vegetable or chicken broth, diced tomatoes (with their juices), smoked paprika, and dried thyme. Bring to a boil.
6. Reduce heat to medium-low and simmer, uncovered, for about 15-20 minutes to allow flavors to meld.
7. Using an immersion blender, blend the soup until smooth. Alternatively, carefully transfer the soup in batches to a blender and blend until smooth, then return to the pot.
8. Stir in heavy cream (if using) and season with salt and pepper to taste.
9. Simmer for another 5 minutes to heat through and blend flavors.
10. Serve hot, garnished with chopped fresh basil or parsley.

Roasted Red Pepper Soup is vibrant, smoky, and perfect for a comforting meal. Enjoy the rich flavors and silky texture of this homemade soup!

Carrot Ginger Soup

Ingredients:

- 2 tablespoons olive oil
- 1 onion, chopped
- 2 cloves garlic, minced
- 1 tablespoon fresh ginger, grated
- 1 lb carrots, peeled and chopped
- 4 cups vegetable or chicken broth
- 1 can (14 oz) coconut milk
- 1 teaspoon ground cumin
- 1/2 teaspoon ground coriander
- Salt and pepper to taste
- Fresh cilantro, chopped, for garnish

Instructions:

1. In a large pot or Dutch oven, heat olive oil over medium heat. Add chopped onion and cook until softened, about 5 minutes.
2. Add minced garlic and grated ginger. Cook for another minute until fragrant.
3. Stir in chopped carrots and cook for 5 minutes, stirring occasionally.
4. Pour in vegetable or chicken broth. Bring to a boil, then reduce heat to medium-low and simmer, uncovered, for about 20-25 minutes or until carrots are tender.
5. Using an immersion blender, blend the soup until smooth. Alternatively, carefully transfer the soup in batches to a blender and blend until smooth, then return to the pot.
6. Stir in coconut milk, ground cumin, and ground coriander. Season with salt and pepper to taste.
7. Simmer for another 5 minutes to heat through and blend flavors.
8. Taste and adjust seasoning if needed.
9. Serve hot, garnished with chopped fresh cilantro.

Carrot Ginger Soup is creamy, aromatic, and packed with wholesome flavors. Enjoy the comforting warmth and soothing qualities of this homemade soup!

Hungarian Mushroom Soup

Ingredients:

- 2 tablespoons unsalted butter
- 1 onion, finely chopped
- 2 cloves garlic, minced
- 1 lb mushrooms (such as cremini or button), sliced
- 1 tablespoon sweet paprika
- 1 teaspoon smoked paprika (optional, for added depth)
- 4 cups vegetable or chicken broth
- 1 cup sour cream
- 1/4 cup all-purpose flour
- 1/2 cup milk
- Salt and pepper to taste
- Fresh parsley, chopped, for garnish

Instructions:

1. In a large pot or Dutch oven, melt butter over medium heat. Add finely chopped onion and cook until softened, about 5 minutes.
2. Add minced garlic and sliced mushrooms to the pot. Cook for about 8-10 minutes, stirring occasionally, until mushrooms are softened and browned.
3. Stir in sweet paprika and smoked paprika (if using). Cook for another 1-2 minutes until fragrant.
4. Pour in vegetable or chicken broth. Bring to a boil, then reduce heat to medium-low and simmer, uncovered, for about 15-20 minutes, stirring occasionally.
5. In a small bowl, whisk together sour cream, flour, and milk until smooth.
6. Gradually stir the sour cream mixture into the soup. Cook for another 5-7 minutes, stirring constantly, until soup is thickened and creamy.
7. Season with salt and pepper to taste.
8. Remove from heat.
9. Serve hot, garnished with chopped fresh parsley.

Hungarian Mushroom Soup is creamy, savory, and full of robust mushroom flavor with a hint of paprika. Enjoy the comforting richness of this homemade soup!

Egg Drop Soup

Ingredients:

- 4 cups chicken broth
- 2 tablespoons soy sauce
- 1 teaspoon sesame oil
- 1/2 teaspoon ground ginger (optional)
- 2 green onions, thinly sliced (white and green parts separated)
- 2 eggs, lightly beaten
- Salt and white pepper to taste
- Fresh cilantro or parsley, chopped, for garnish (optional)

Instructions:

1. In a large pot, bring chicken broth to a boil over medium-high heat.
2. Stir in soy sauce, sesame oil, ground ginger (if using), and the white parts of the green onions. Reduce heat to medium-low and simmer for about 5 minutes to allow flavors to meld.
3. While the broth is simmering, slowly pour the beaten eggs into the soup in a steady stream, stirring gently with a fork or chopsticks in one direction. This will create the characteristic egg ribbons in the soup.
4. Cook for another 1-2 minutes, until the eggs are set.
5. Season with salt and white pepper to taste.
6. Remove from heat.
7. Ladle into bowls and garnish with the green parts of the green onions and chopped cilantro or parsley (if using).

Egg Drop Soup is light, flavorful, and perfect for a quick and comforting meal. Enjoy the delicate egg ribbons and savory broth in this homemade soup!

Thai Coconut Soup

Ingredients:

- 1 tablespoon vegetable oil
- 1 onion, thinly sliced
- 2 cloves garlic, minced
- 1 tablespoon fresh ginger, grated
- 2-3 tablespoons Thai red curry paste (adjust to taste)
- 4 cups chicken or vegetable broth
- 1 can (14 oz) coconut milk
- 1 tablespoon soy sauce
- 1 tablespoon fish sauce (optional, for authentic Thai flavor)
- 1 tablespoon brown sugar
- 1 lb boneless, skinless chicken thighs or breasts, thinly sliced
- 8 oz mushrooms, sliced
- 1 red bell pepper, thinly sliced
- Juice of 1 lime
- Salt and pepper to taste
- Fresh cilantro or Thai basil, chopped, for garnish
- Red pepper flakes or sliced red chilies, for garnish (optional)

Instructions:

1. In a large pot or Dutch oven, heat vegetable oil over medium heat. Add thinly sliced onion and cook for 5 minutes until softened.
2. Add minced garlic, grated ginger, and Thai red curry paste. Cook for another 1-2 minutes until fragrant.
3. Pour in chicken or vegetable broth and bring to a boil.
4. Reduce heat to medium-low and stir in coconut milk, soy sauce, fish sauce (if using), and brown sugar. Simmer for 5 minutes, stirring occasionally.
5. Add thinly sliced chicken, mushrooms, and red bell pepper to the pot. Simmer for 10-15 minutes or until chicken is cooked through and vegetables are tender.
6. Stir in lime juice. Season with salt and pepper to taste.
7. Remove from heat.
8. Serve hot, garnished with chopped fresh cilantro or Thai basil, and red pepper flakes or sliced red chilies if desired.

Thai Coconut Soup is creamy, fragrant, and bursting with Thai flavors. Enjoy the combination of coconut milk, Thai curry paste, and aromatic herbs in this comforting and flavorful soup!

Avgolemono Soup

Ingredients:

- 8 cups chicken broth
- 1/2 cup Arborio rice or orzo pasta
- 3 eggs
- Juice of 2-3 lemons (about 1/2 to 3/4 cup)
- Salt and pepper to taste
- Fresh dill, chopped, for garnish (optional)

Instructions:

1. In a large pot, bring chicken broth to a boil over medium-high heat.
2. Add Arborio rice or orzo pasta to the pot. Reduce heat to medium-low and simmer for about 15-20 minutes, or until rice or pasta is cooked through and tender.
3. In a mixing bowl, whisk together eggs and lemon juice until smooth and frothy.
4. Slowly ladle about 1 cup of the hot broth from the pot into the egg-lemon mixture, whisking constantly. This tempers the eggs so they don't curdle when added to the soup.
5. Gradually pour the egg-lemon mixture back into the pot, stirring constantly to incorporate.
6. Cook over low heat for another 5 minutes, stirring occasionally, until the soup thickens slightly. Do not let it boil, as this can cause the eggs to curdle.
7. Season with salt and pepper to taste.
8. Remove from heat.
9. Serve hot, garnished with chopped fresh dill if desired.

Avgolemono Soup is creamy, tangy, and comforting with a refreshing lemon flavor. Enjoy this traditional Greek soup as a light and satisfying meal!

Navy Bean Soup

Ingredients:

- 1 lb dried navy beans, rinsed and picked over
- 1 tablespoon olive oil
- 1 onion, chopped
- 2 carrots, diced
- 2 celery stalks, diced
- 3 cloves garlic, minced
- 8 cups chicken or vegetable broth
- 1 bay leaf
- 1 teaspoon dried thyme
- 1 teaspoon dried oregano
- Salt and pepper to taste
- Optional: 1 ham hock or 1 cup diced ham
- Fresh parsley, chopped, for garnish (optional)

Instructions:

1. In a large pot or Dutch oven, heat olive oil over medium heat. Add chopped onion, diced carrots, and diced celery. Cook for about 5-7 minutes, until vegetables are softened.
2. Add minced garlic and cook for another minute until fragrant.
3. Stir in dried navy beans, chicken or vegetable broth, bay leaf, dried thyme, and dried oregano. If using a ham hock or diced ham, add it to the pot.
4. Bring the mixture to a boil, then reduce heat to medium-low and simmer, partially covered, for about 1.5 to 2 hours, or until beans are tender. Stir occasionally and add more broth or water if needed.
5. Once beans are tender and the soup has thickened, remove the ham hock (if used) and bay leaf. If using diced ham, it should be tender and infused with flavor.
6. Season with salt and pepper to taste.
7. Remove from heat.
8. Serve hot, garnished with chopped fresh parsley if desired.

Navy Bean Soup is hearty, nutritious, and perfect for a comforting meal, especially on cooler days. Enjoy the rich flavors of beans and vegetables in this homemade soup!

Creamy Chicken and Mushroom Soup

Ingredients:

- 2 tablespoons butter
- 1 lb boneless, skinless chicken breasts, cut into bite-sized pieces
- Salt and pepper to taste
- 1 onion, chopped
- 2 cloves garlic, minced
- 8 oz mushrooms (such as cremini or button), sliced
- 1 teaspoon dried thyme
- 4 cups chicken broth
- 1 cup heavy cream
- 1/4 cup all-purpose flour
- Fresh parsley, chopped, for garnish

Instructions:

1. In a large pot or Dutch oven, melt butter over medium-high heat. Season chicken pieces with salt and pepper, then add them to the pot. Cook until chicken is browned and cooked through, about 5-7 minutes. Remove chicken from the pot and set aside.
2. In the same pot, add chopped onion and cook for 3-4 minutes until softened. Add minced garlic and cook for another minute until fragrant.
3. Add sliced mushrooms and dried thyme to the pot. Cook for 5-7 minutes until mushrooms are softened and browned.
4. Pour in chicken broth and bring to a boil. Reduce heat to medium-low and simmer for about 10 minutes.
5. In a small bowl, whisk together heavy cream and flour until smooth. Slowly pour the cream mixture into the pot, stirring constantly to prevent lumps from forming.
6. Add cooked chicken back to the pot. Simmer for another 5-7 minutes until soup has thickened slightly and chicken is heated through.
7. Season with salt and pepper to taste.
8. Remove from heat.
9. Serve hot, garnished with chopped fresh parsley.

Creamy Chicken and Mushroom Soup is rich, flavorful, and perfect for a comforting meal. Enjoy the hearty combination of chicken, mushrooms, and creamy broth in this homemade soup!

Hawaiian Beef Soup

Ingredients:

- 2 tablespoons vegetable oil
- 1.5 lbs beef stew meat, cut into bite-sized pieces
- 1 onion, chopped
- 3 cloves garlic, minced
- 4 cups beef broth
- 2 cups water
- 2 large carrots, peeled and sliced
- 2 large potatoes, peeled and diced
- 1 cup celery, sliced
- 1 cup green beans, trimmed and cut into 1-inch pieces
- 1 can (14.5 oz) diced tomatoes
- 1 tablespoon soy sauce
- 1 tablespoon Worcestershire sauce
- 1 tablespoon tomato paste
- 1 bay leaf
- Salt and pepper to taste
- Green onions, chopped, for garnish

Instructions:

1. In a large pot or Dutch oven, heat vegetable oil over medium-high heat. Add beef stew meat and cook until browned on all sides, about 5-7 minutes. Remove beef from the pot and set aside.
2. In the same pot, add chopped onion and cook for 3-4 minutes until softened. Add minced garlic and cook for another minute until fragrant.
3. Return the browned beef to the pot. Pour in beef broth and water. Bring to a boil, then reduce heat to medium-low and simmer, covered, for 1.5 to 2 hours or until beef is tender.
4. Add sliced carrots, diced potatoes, sliced celery, green beans, diced tomatoes (with their juices), soy sauce, Worcestershire sauce, tomato paste, and bay leaf to the pot. Stir to combine.
5. Simmer, covered, for another 30-45 minutes or until vegetables are tender and flavors have melded.
6. Season with salt and pepper to taste.
7. Remove bay leaf before serving.
8. Serve hot, garnished with chopped green onions.

Hawaiian Beef Soup is hearty, comforting, and full of robust flavors from the beef and vegetables. Enjoy this delicious dish with a touch of Hawaiian influence!